Circle the shape that is the same as the first shape in each row.

Circle the picture that is the same as the first picture in each row.

Draw lines to connect the shapes that are the same.

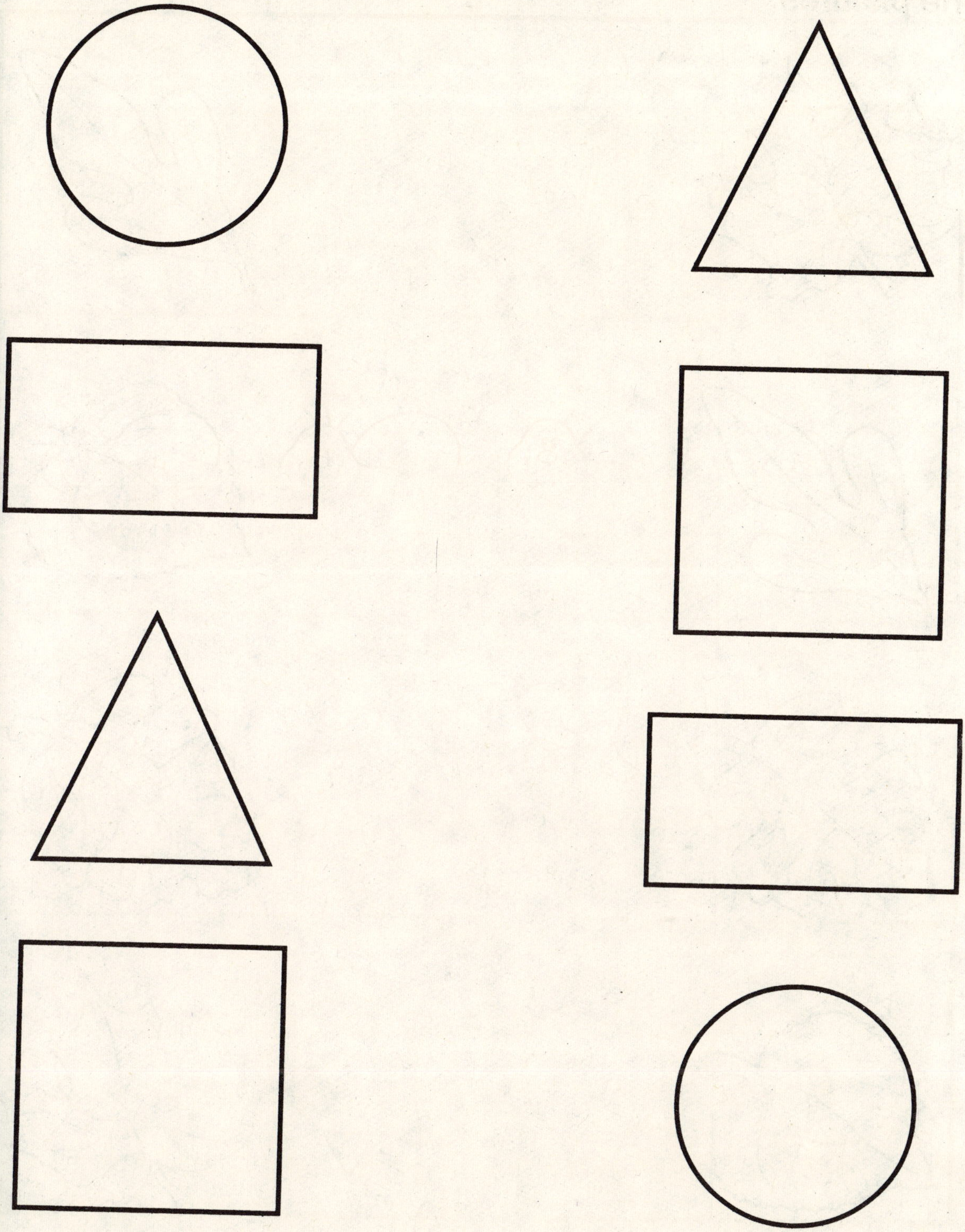

Draw lines to connect the pictures that are the same. Colour the pictures.

Colour the two pictures in each box that are the same.

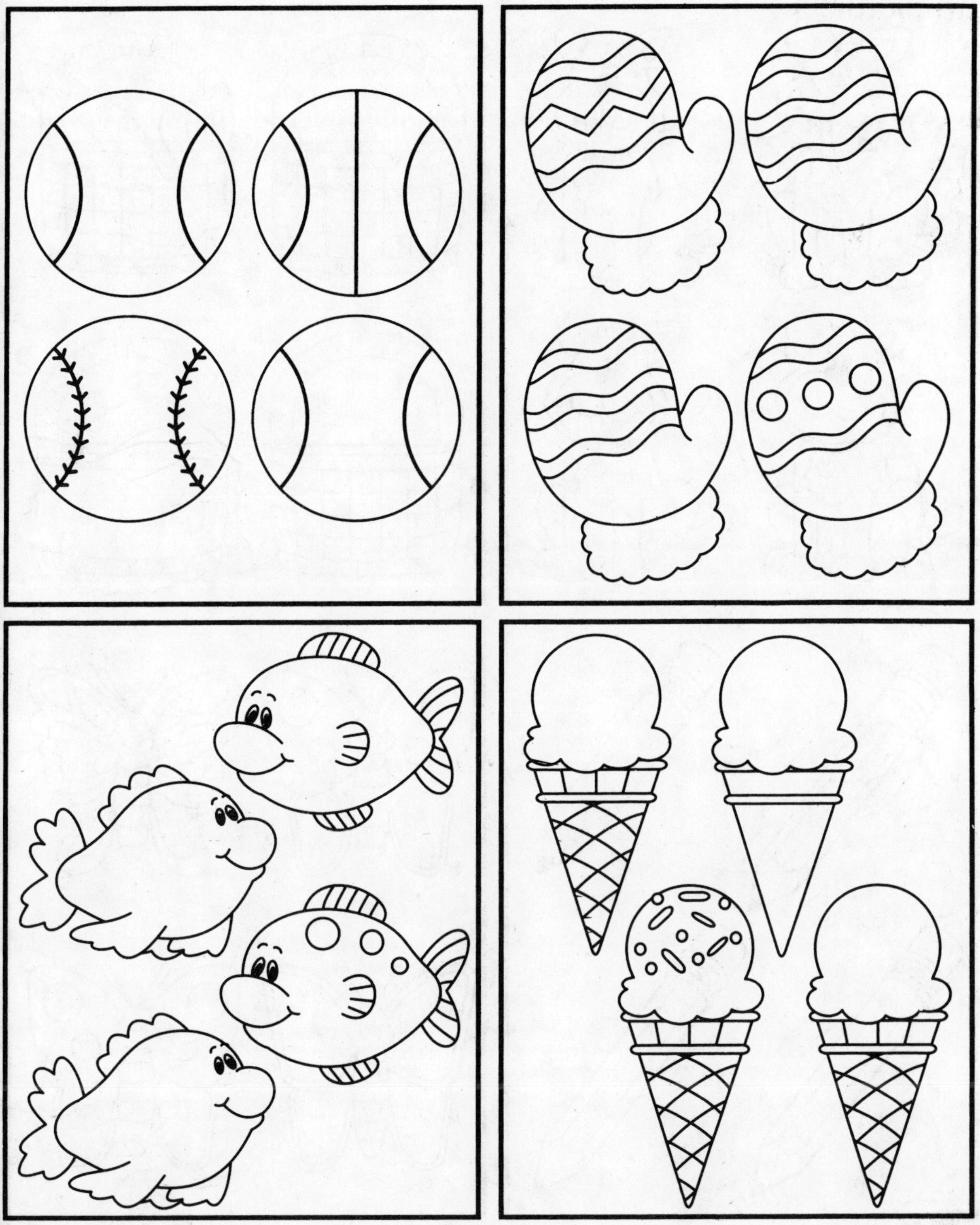

Colour the two pictures in each box that are the same.

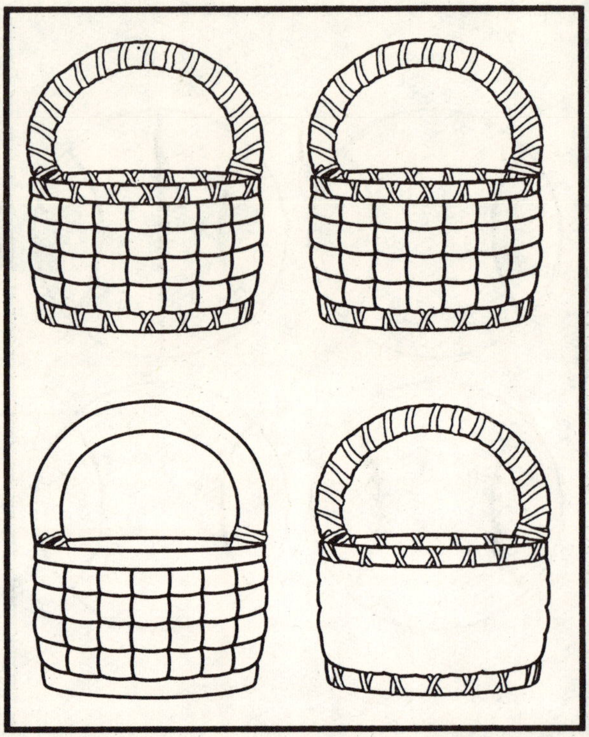

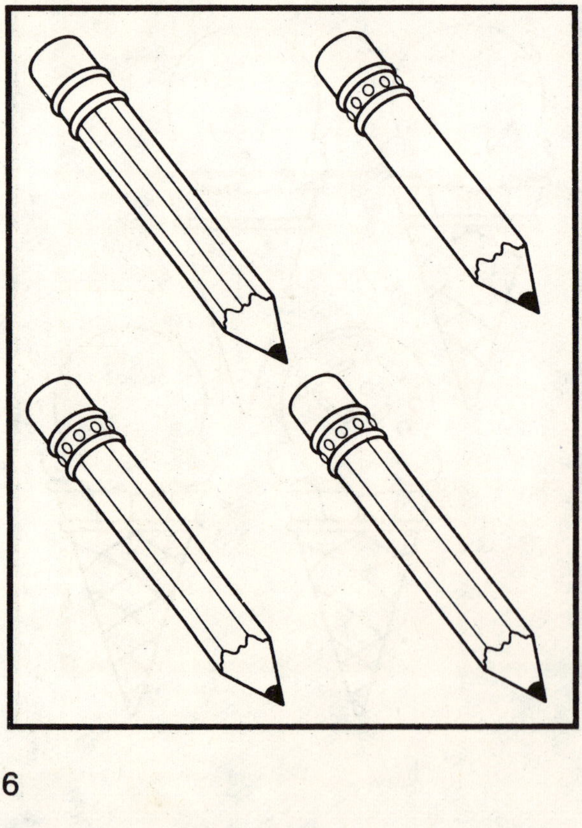

Cut out each shape and paste it beside the shape that is the same. Colour the shapes.

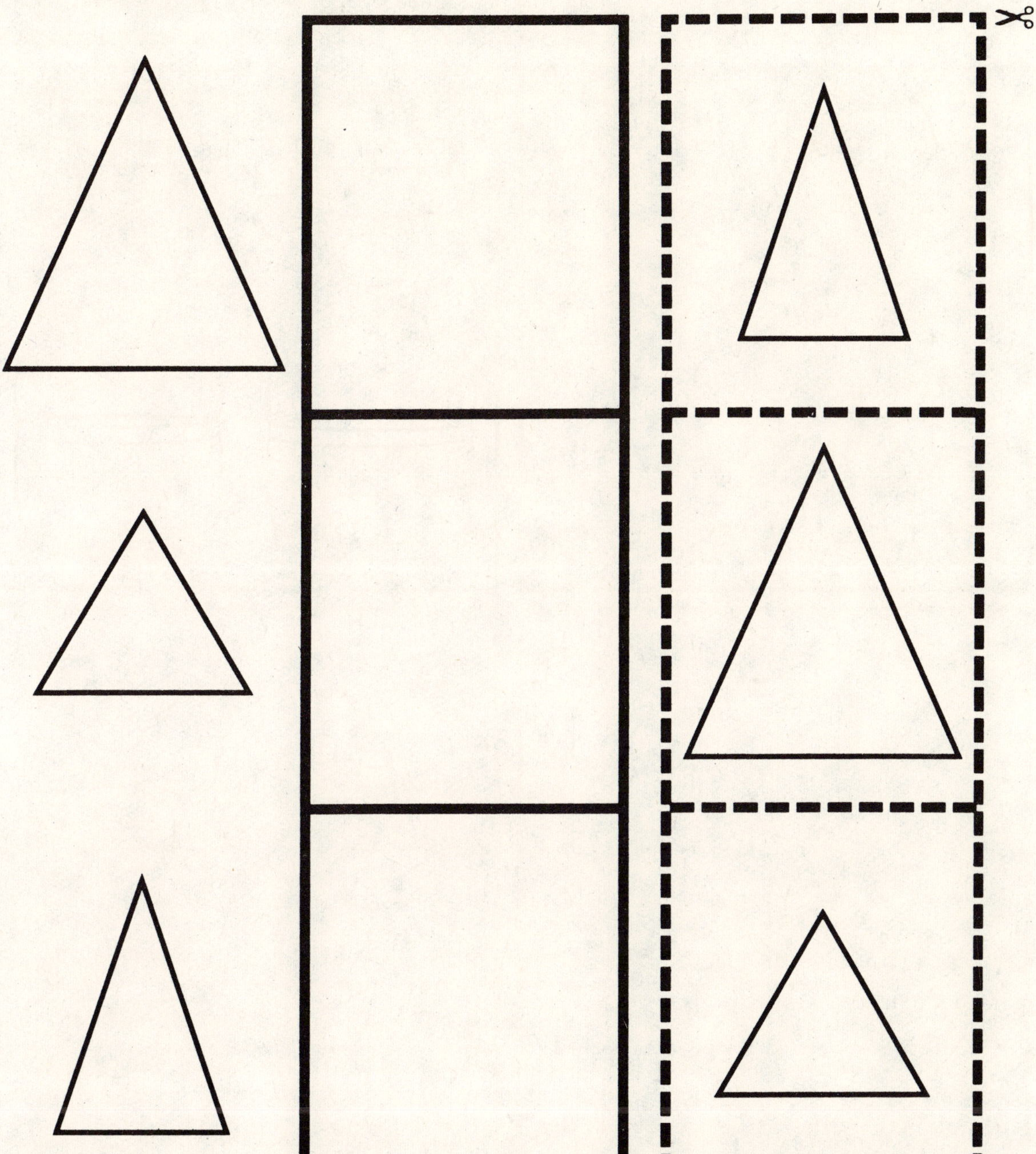

Cut out each shape and paste it in the correct place. Colour the picture.

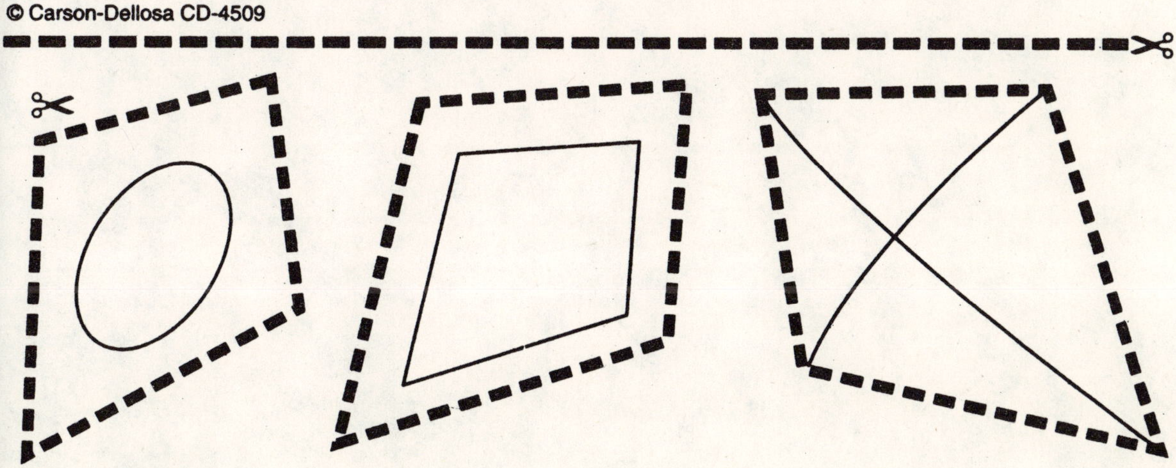

© Carson-Dellosa CD-4509

Look at the first shape in each box. Trace and complete the second shape to look the same. Colour the shapes.

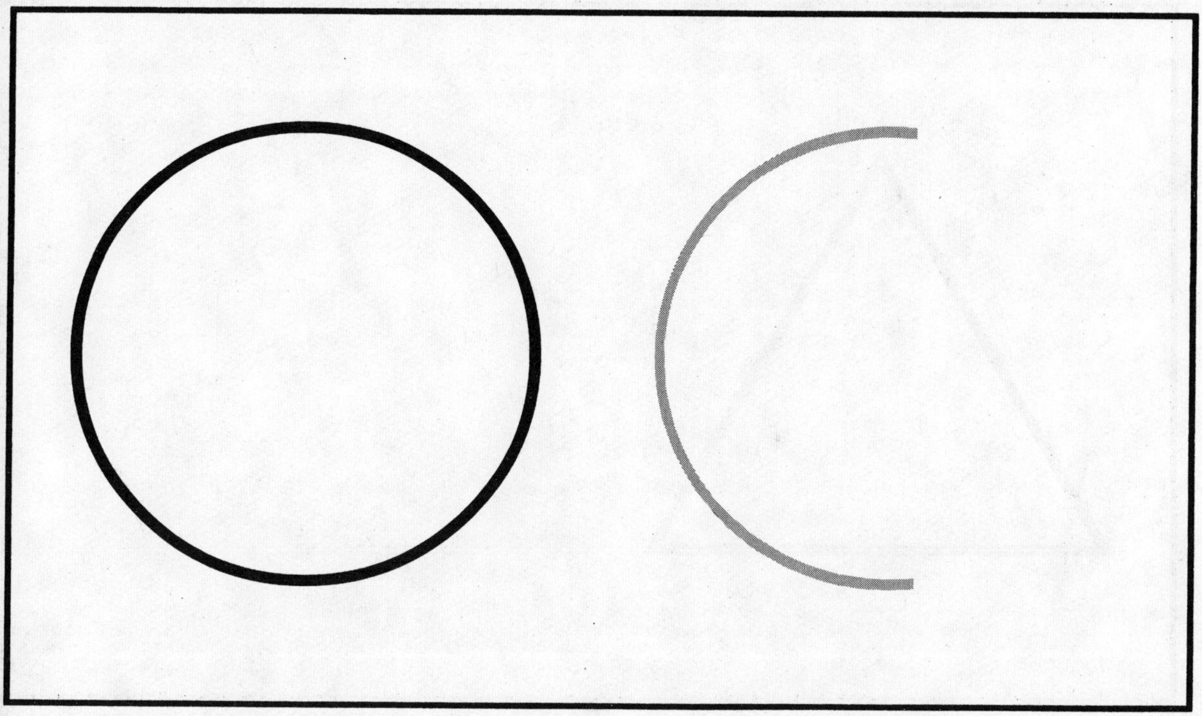

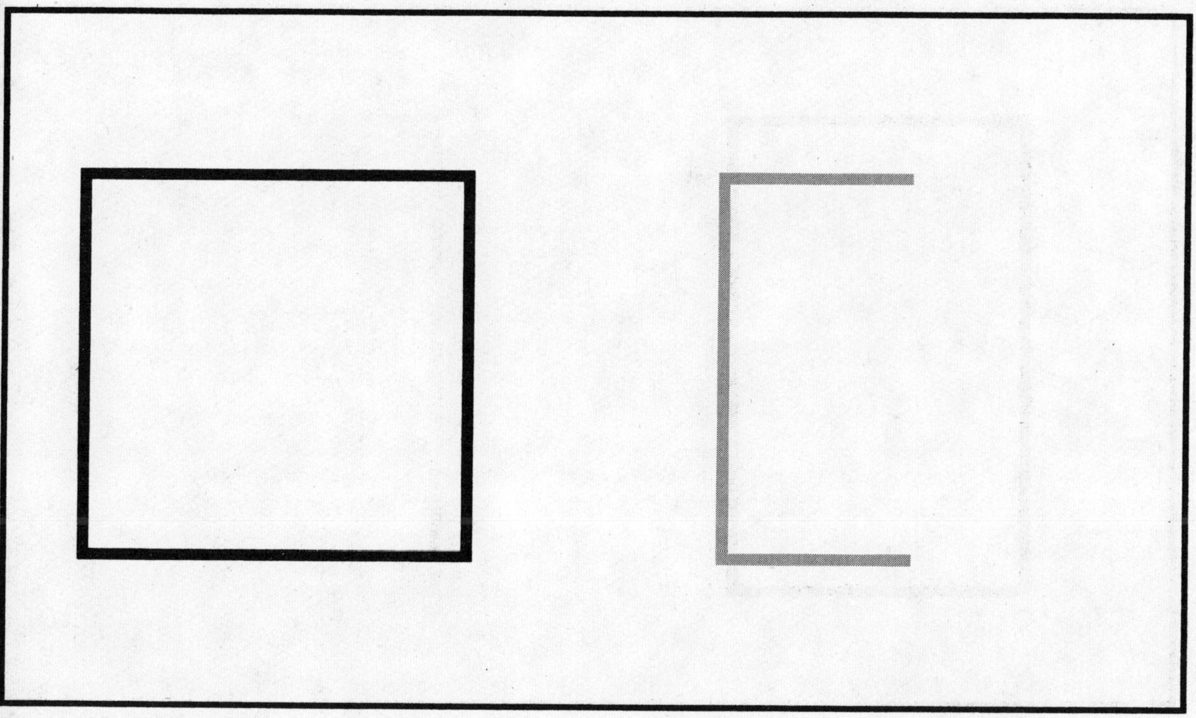

Look at the first shape in each box. Trace and complete the second shape to look the same. Colour the shapes.

Look at the first shape in each box. Trace and complete the second shape to look the same. Colour the shapes.

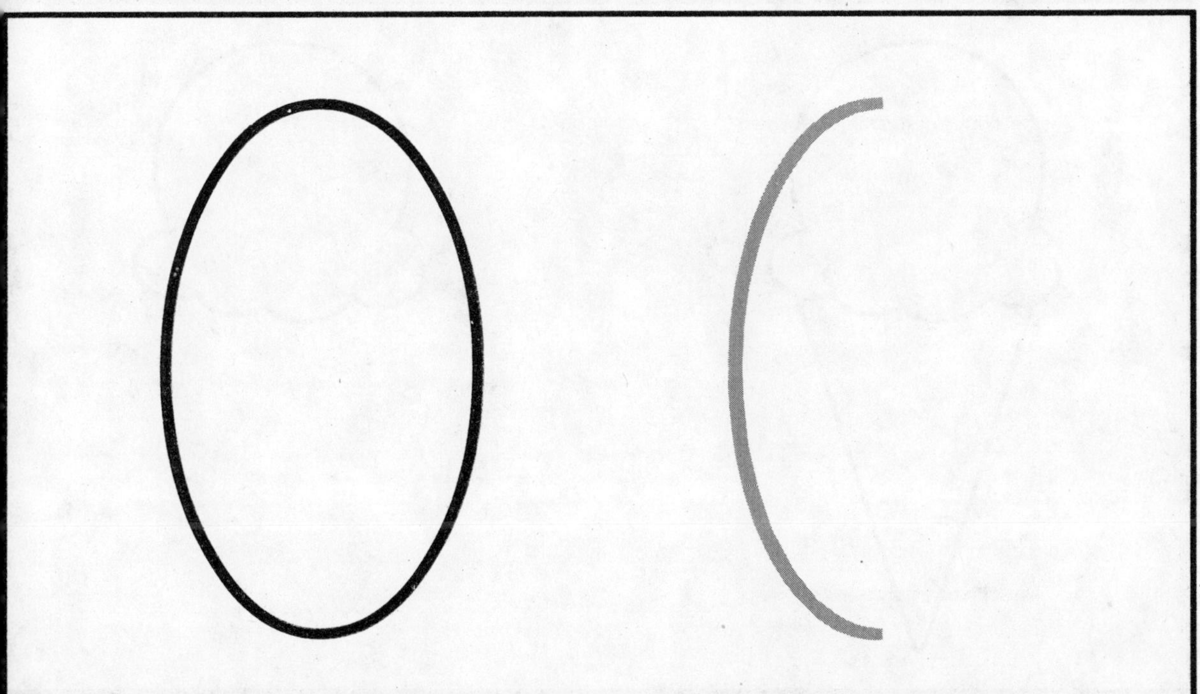

Look at the first picture in each box. Complete the second picture to look the same. Colour the pictures.

Look at the first picture in each box. Complete the second picture to look the same. Colour the pictures.

In each box, draw an X on the shape that is different.

In each box, draw an X on the picture that is different.

Circle the picture in each row that is different.

Cut out each ball and paste it beside the ball that is the same. Colour the pictures.

© Carson-Dellosa CD-4509

Cut out each flower and paste it beside the flower that is the same. Colour the pictures.

© Carson-Dellosa CD-4509

Circle the picture that is the same as the first picture in each row.

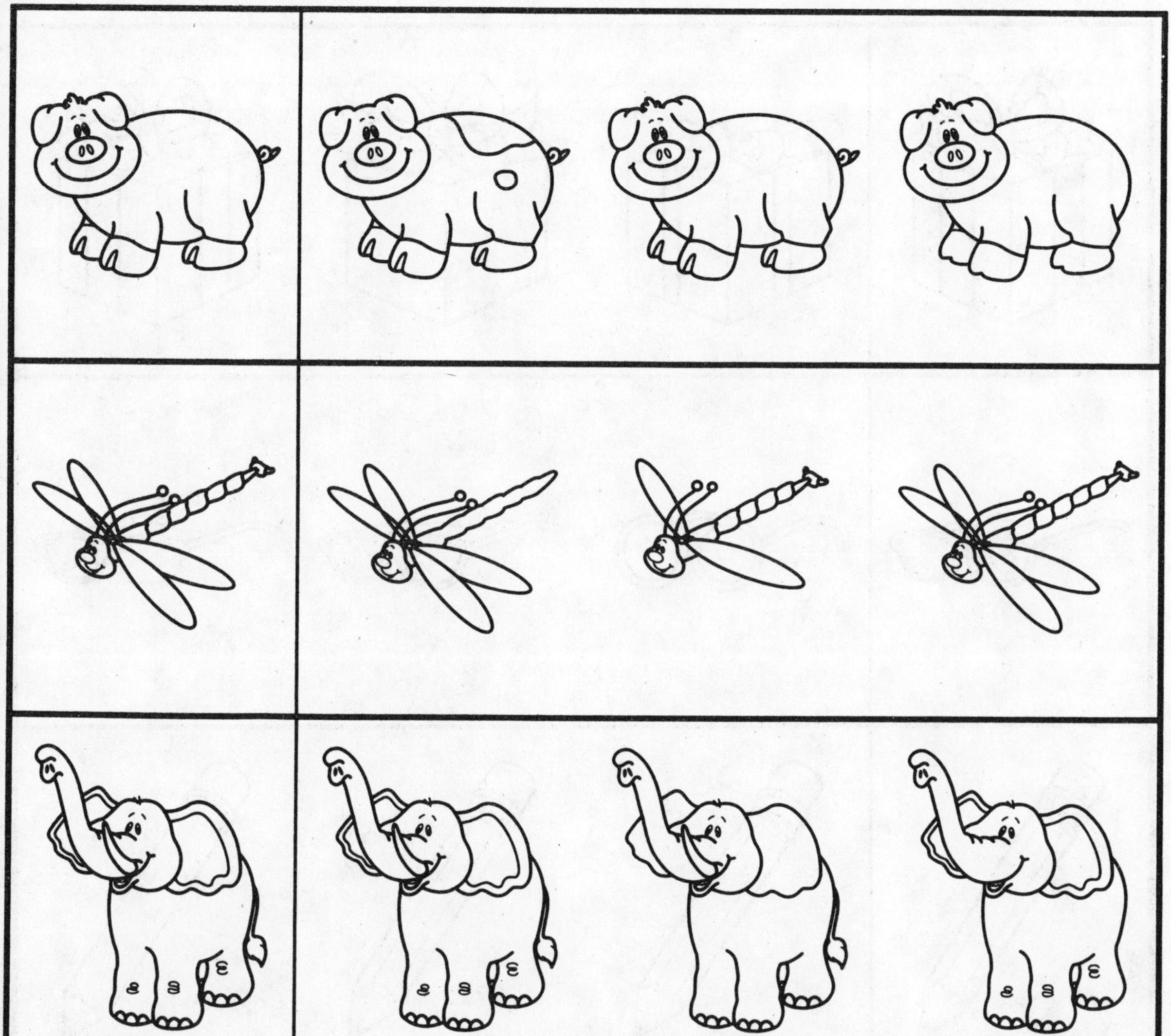

Circle the picture that is the same as the first picture in each row.

Draw lines to connect the pictures that are the same. Colour the pictures.

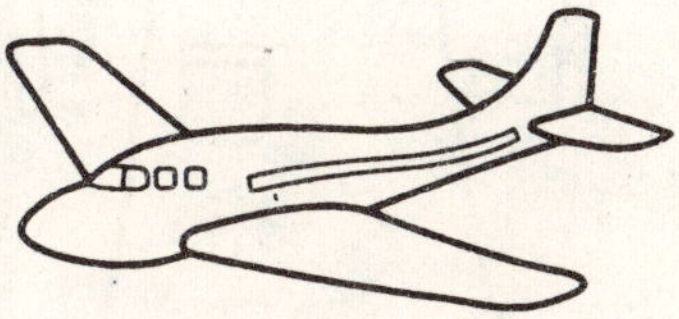

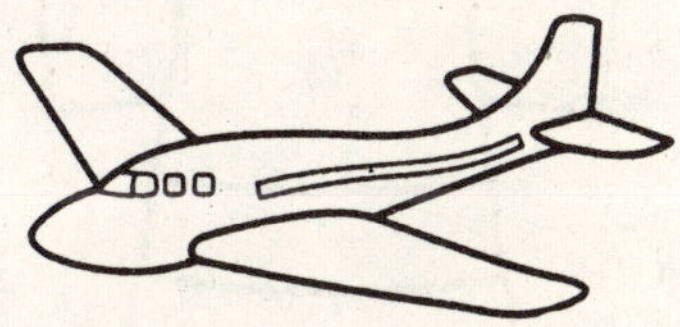

Draw lines to connect the pictures that are the same. Colour the pictures.

Colour the two pictures in each box that are the same.

Colour the two pictures in each row that are the same.

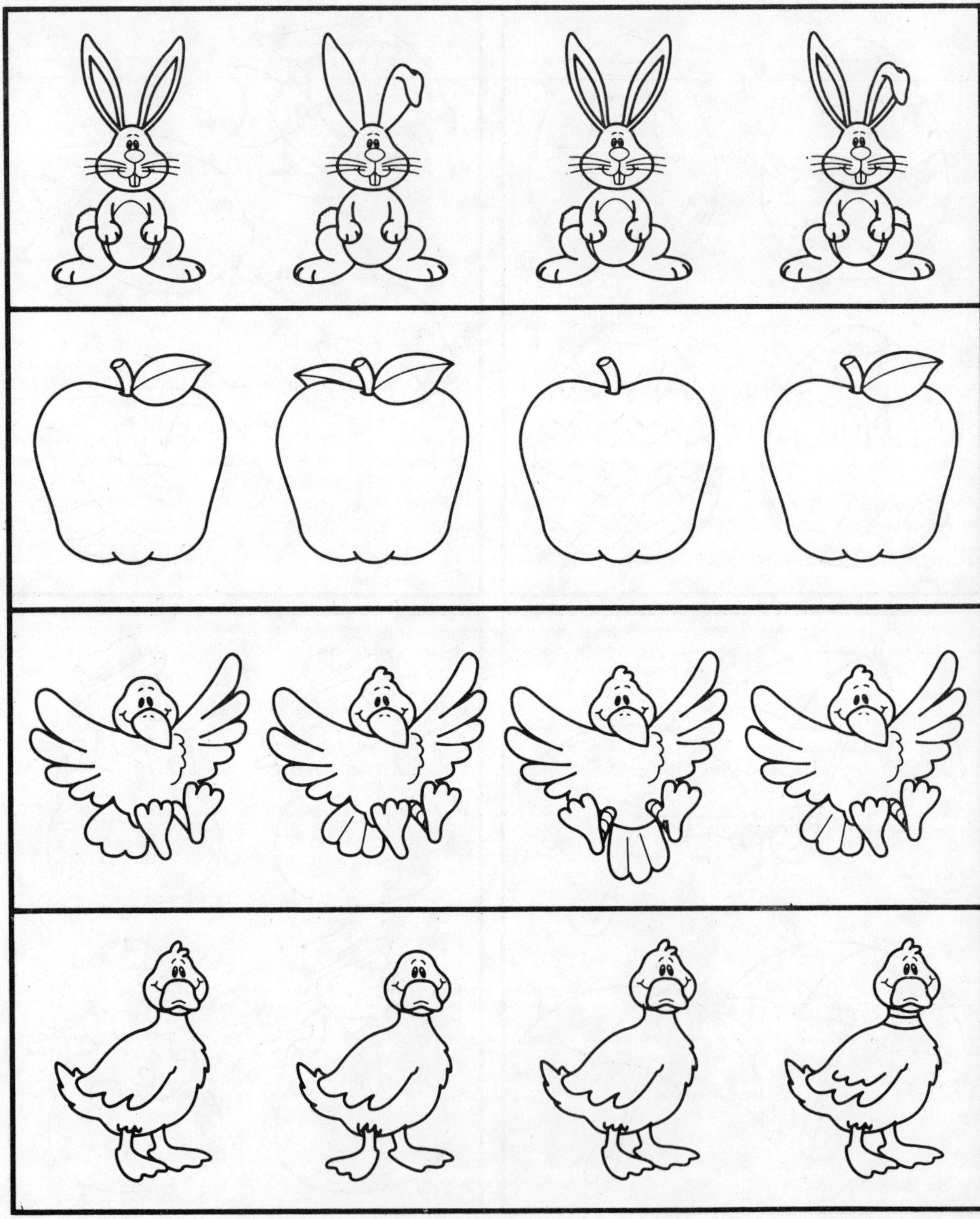

Colour the two pictures in each row that are the same.

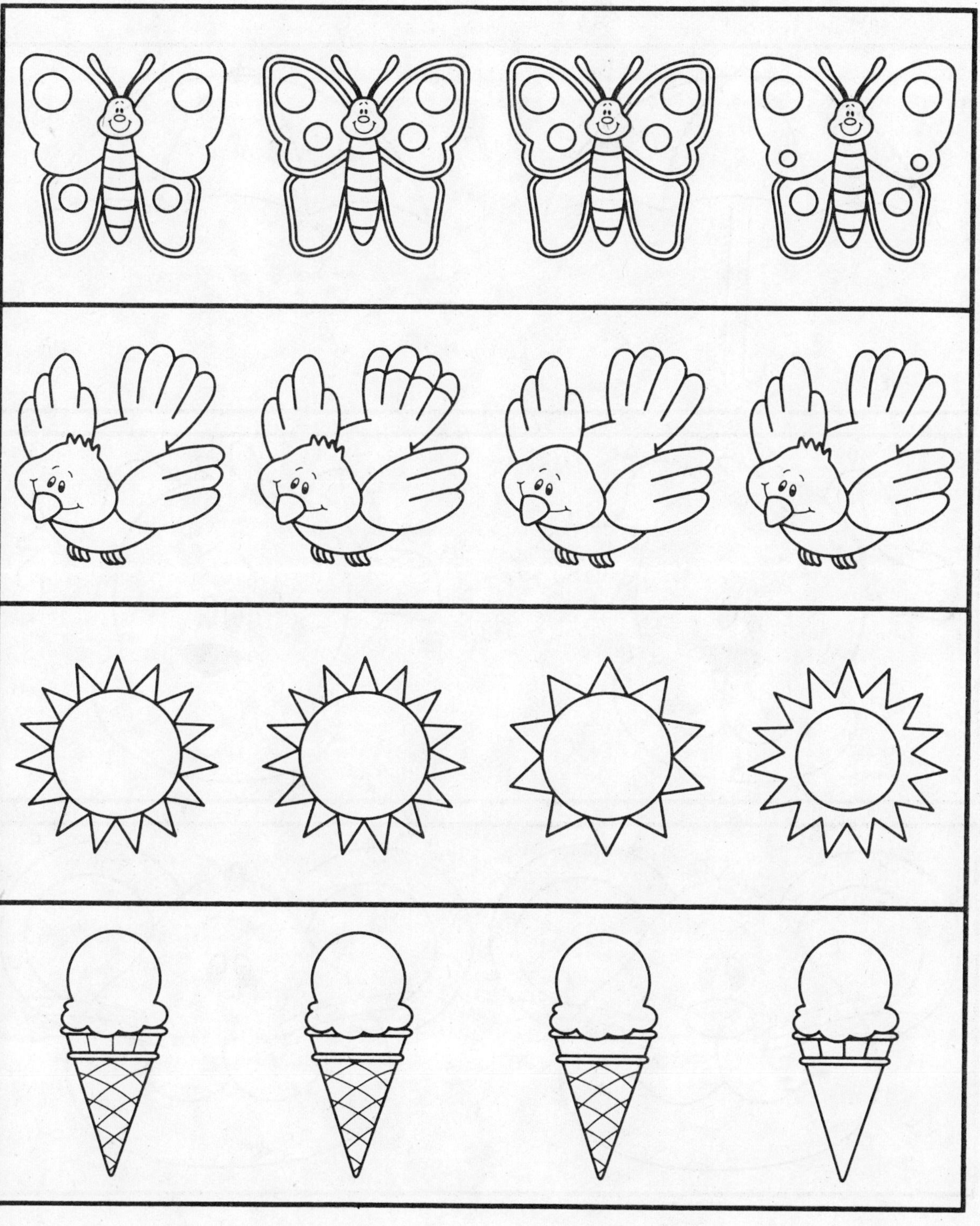

Look at the first picture in each box. Complete the second picture to look the same. Colour the pictures.

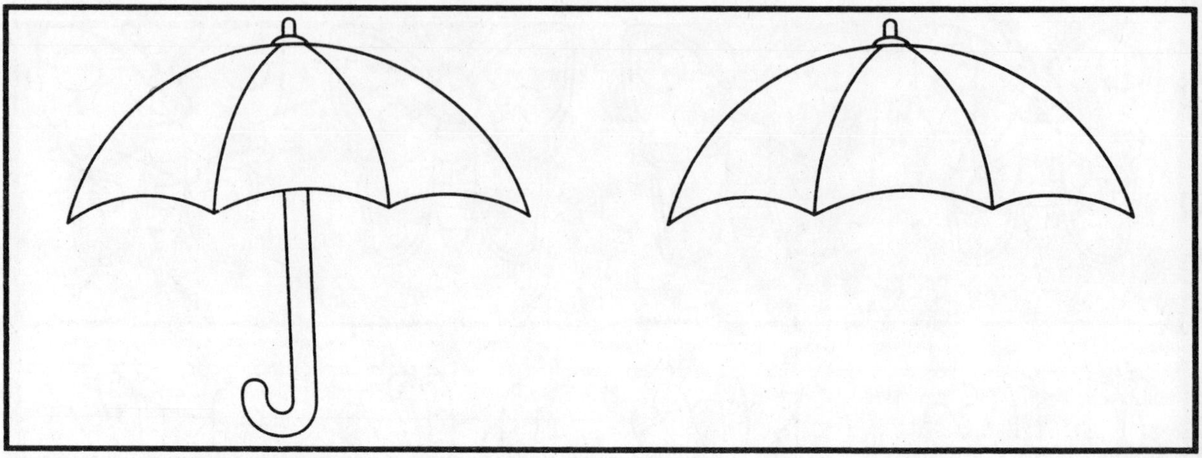

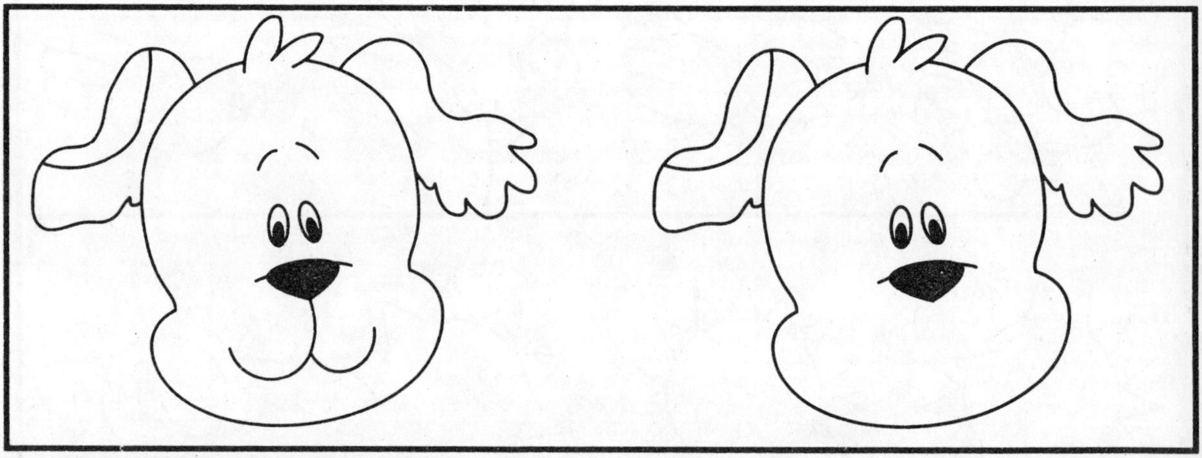

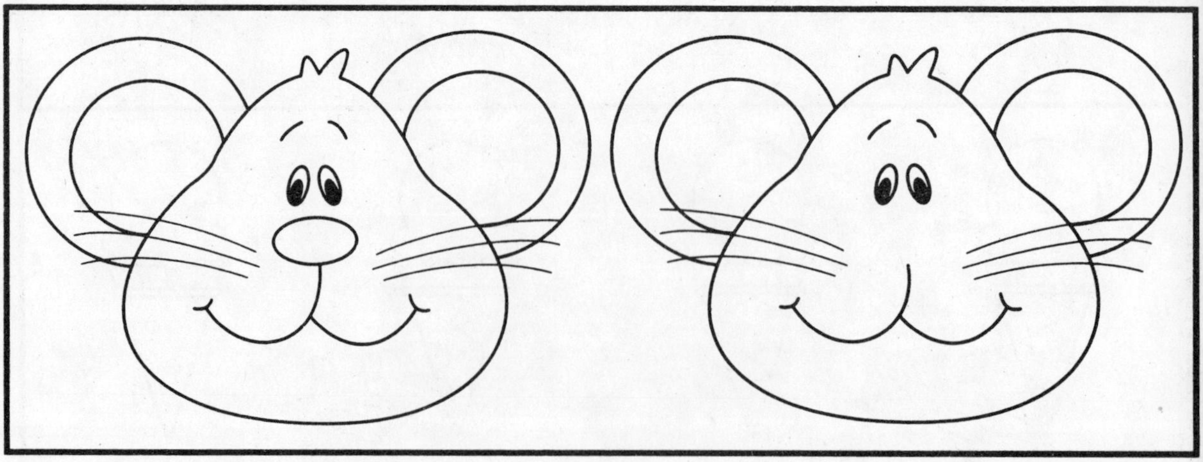

Look at the first picture in each box. Complete the second picture to look the same. Colour the pictures.

Look at the first picture in each box. Complete the second picture to look the same. Colour the pictures.

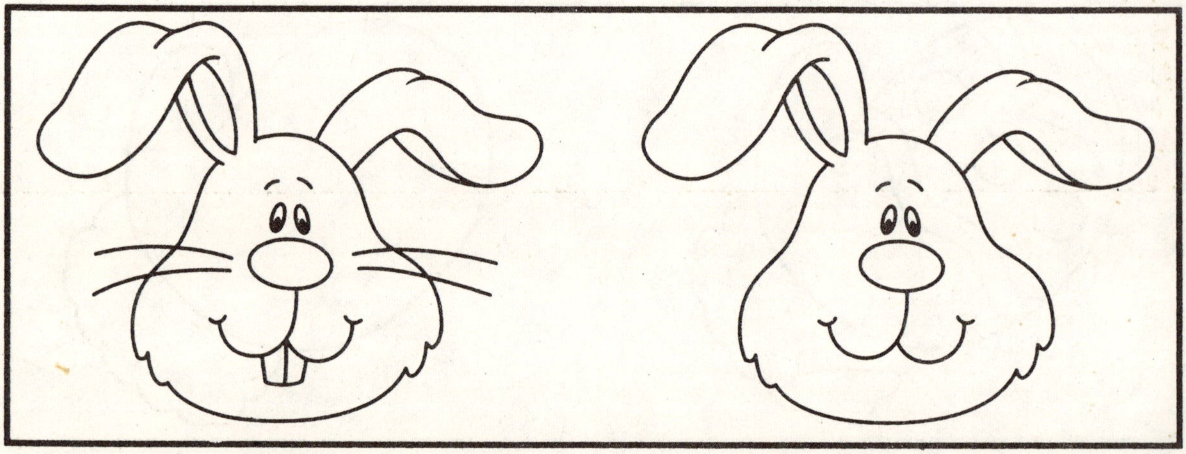

Look at the first picture in each box. Complete the second picture to look the same. Colour the pictures.

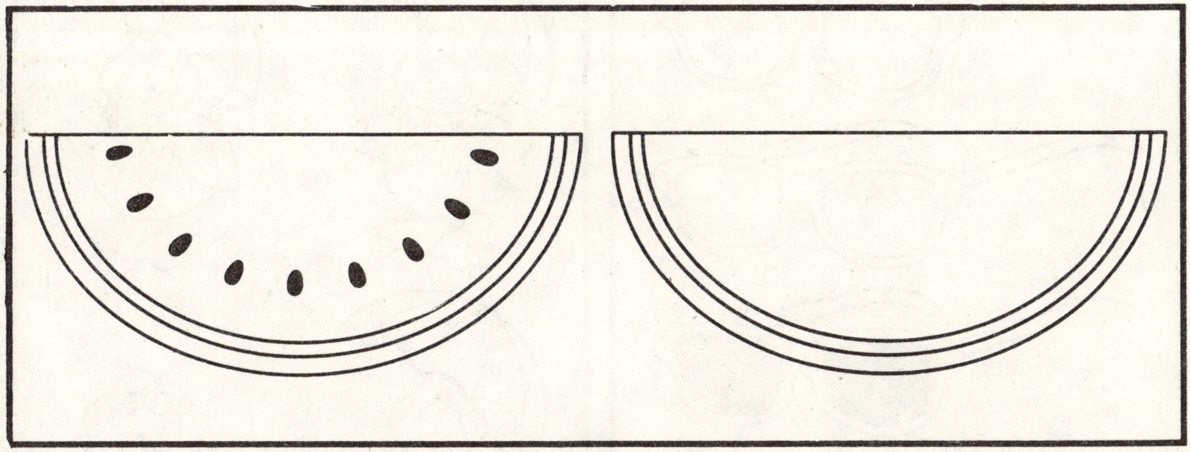

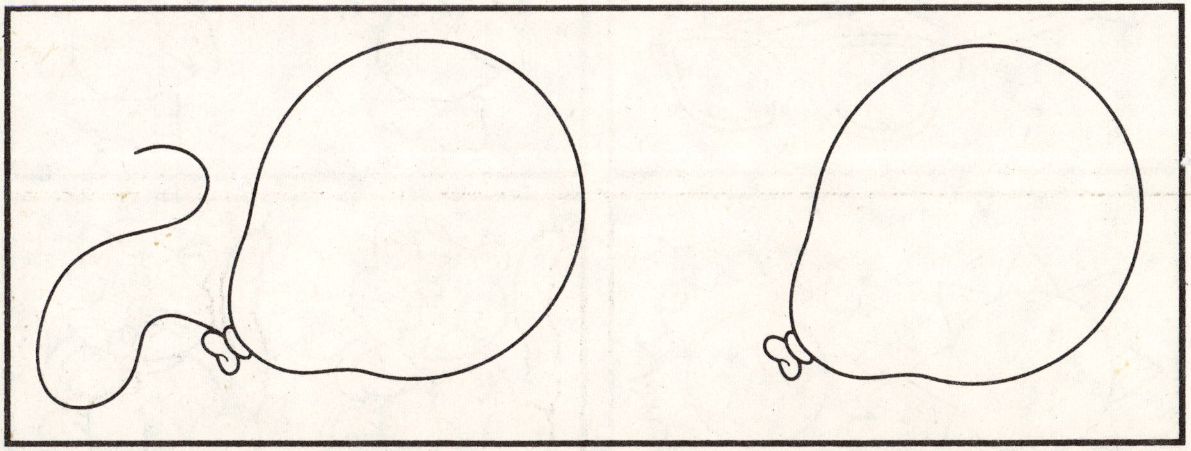

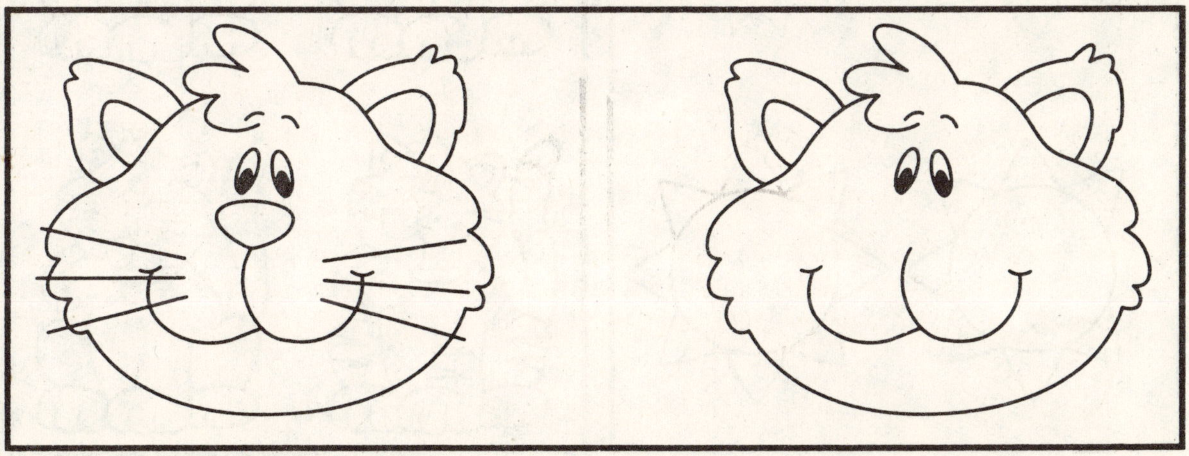

In each box, draw an X on the picture that is different.

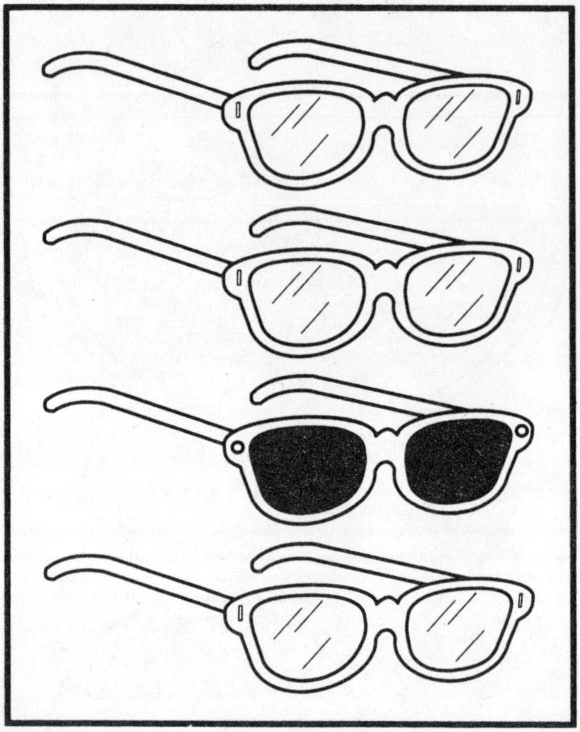

In each box, draw an X on the picture that is different.

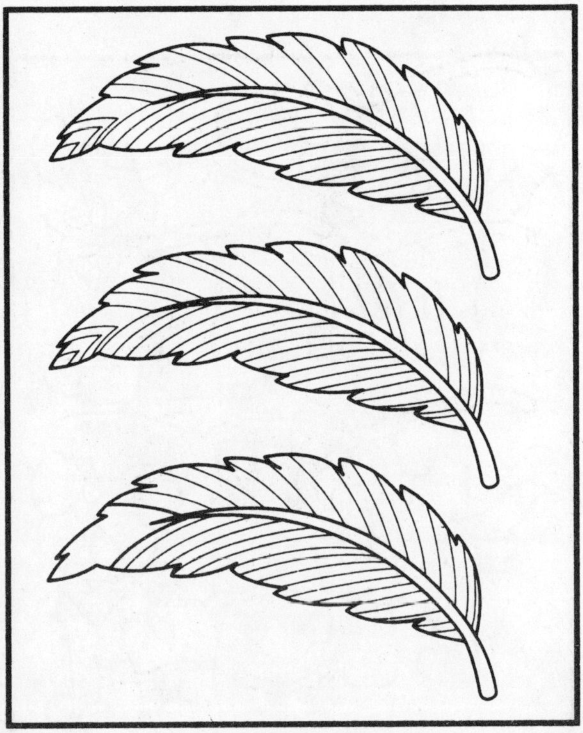

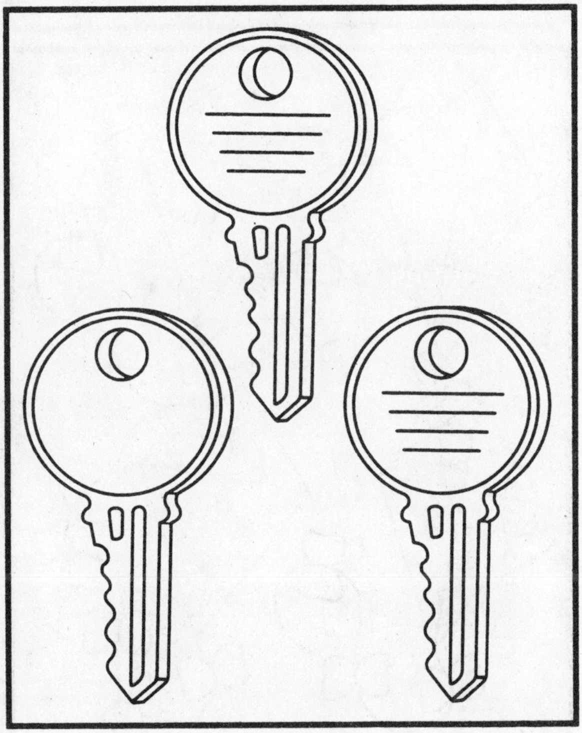

In each box, draw an X on the picture or letter that is different.

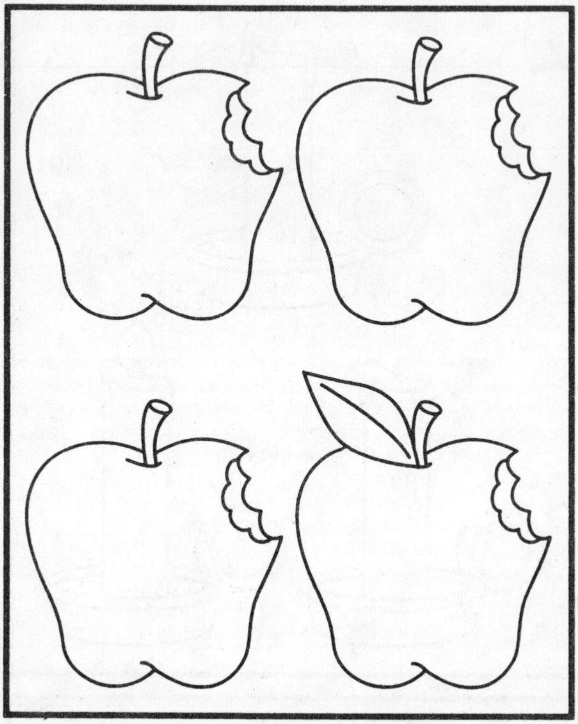

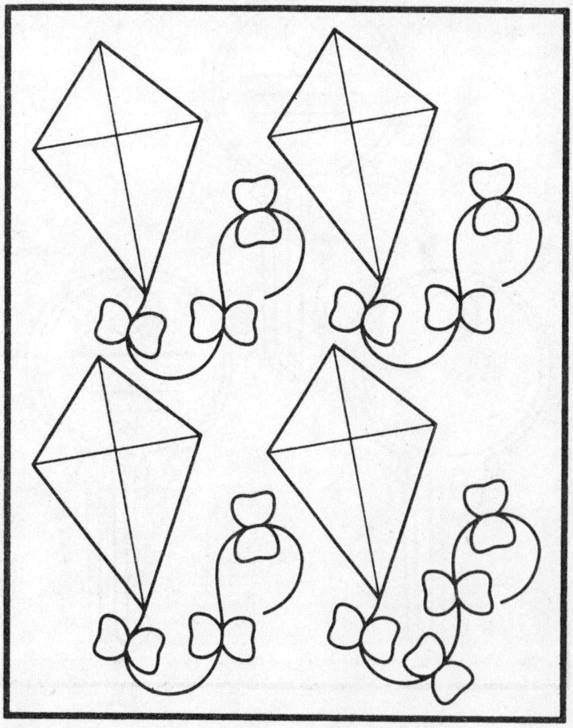

C G

G G

Circle the pictures in each row that are the same. Draw an X on the picture in each row that does not match.

Circle the pictures in each row that are the same. Draw an X on the picture in each row that does not match.

Circle the pictures in each row that are the same. Draw an X on the picture in each row that does not match.

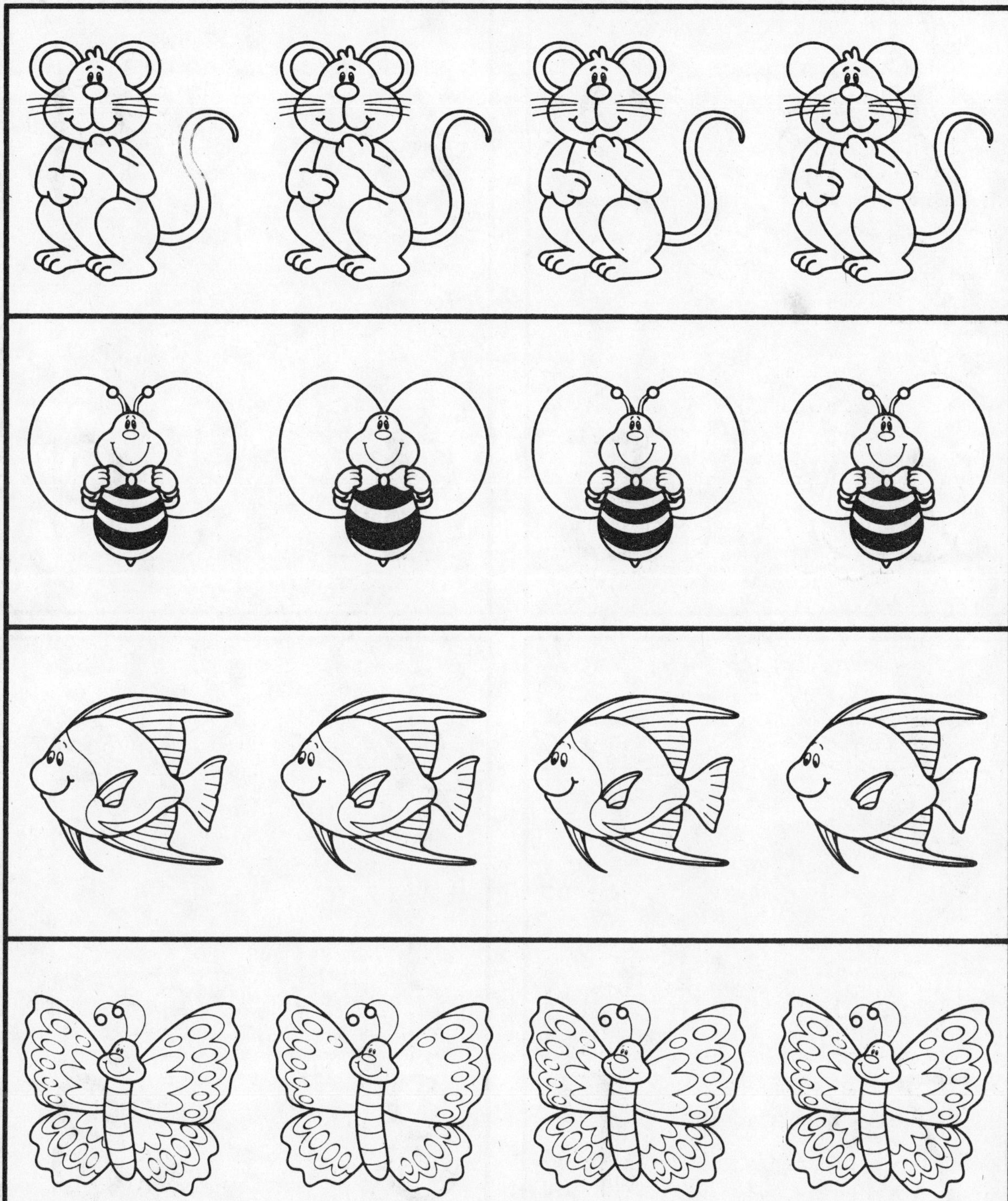

Circle the numbers in each box that are the same. Draw an X on the number in each box that is different.

2	2	6	9
2	5	9	9
7	7	8	3
7	1	3	3

Find and colour the picture that is the same as the picture in the box.

Find and colour the picture that is the same as the picture in the box.

Cut out each part of the house and paste it in the correct place. Colour the picture.

© Carson-Dellosa CD-4509

Cut out each shape and paste it beside the shape that is the same. Colour the shapes.

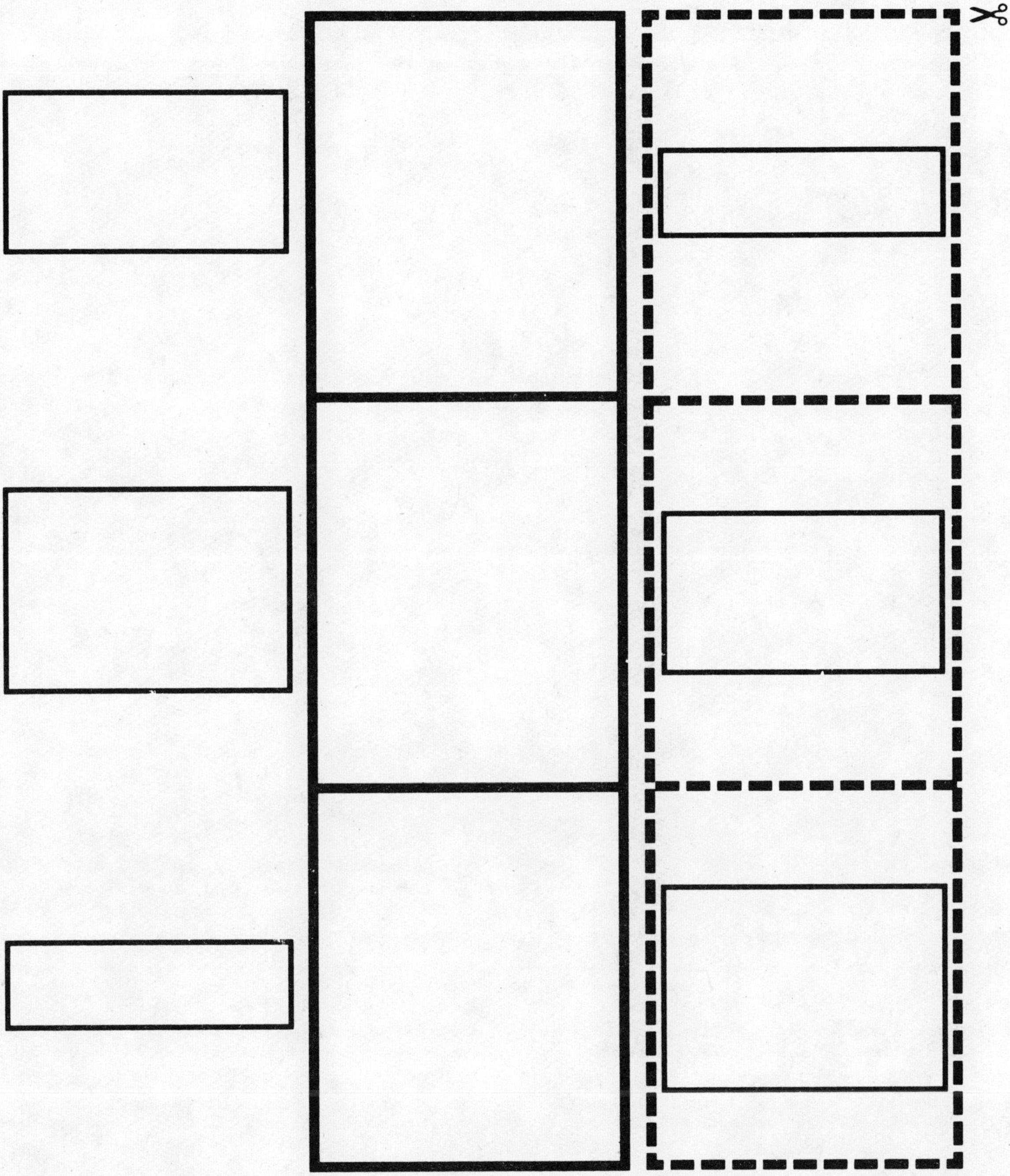

Cut out each letter and paste it beside the letter that is the same.

b

p

a

d

d b p a

© Carson-Dellosa CD-4509

Draw lines to connect the pictures that are the same. Colour the pictures.

Draw lines to connect the pictures that are the same. Colour the pictures.

Draw lines to connect the capital letters that are the same.

Circle the item that matches the first item in each row.

N	M	W	N
			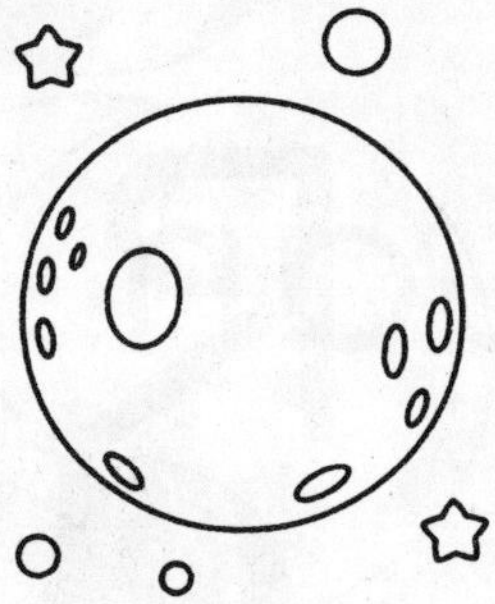
g	q	g	p

Draw lines to connect the words that are the same.

cat

map

pan

can

map

pan

can

cat

Find and Colour the picture that is the same as the picture in the box.

Find and Colour the picture that is the same as the picture in the box.

Look at the first picture in each box. Complete the second picture to look the same. Colour the pictures.

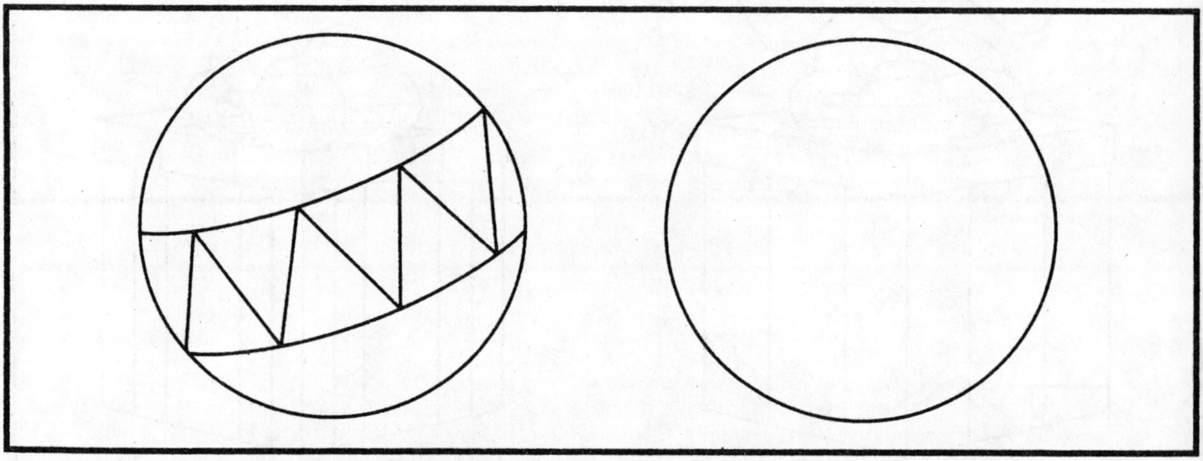

Look at the first picture in each box. Complete the second picture to look the same. Colour the picture.

Draw the other half of each picture to match the first half.
Colour the pictures.

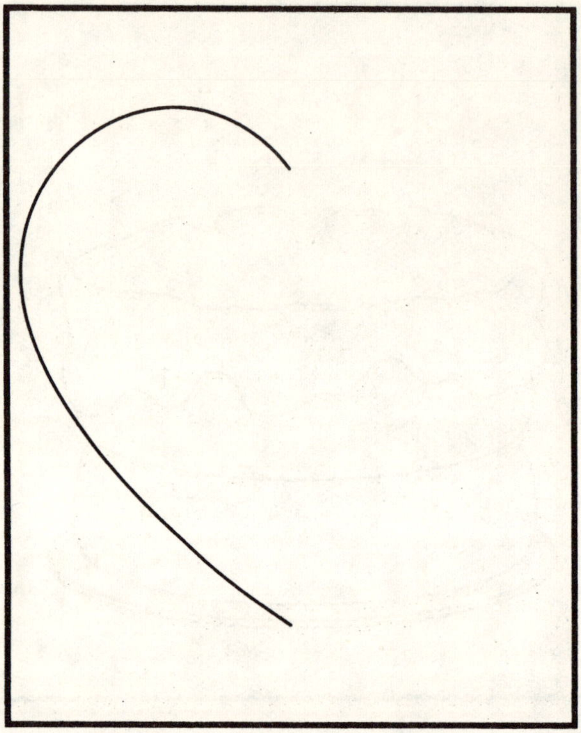

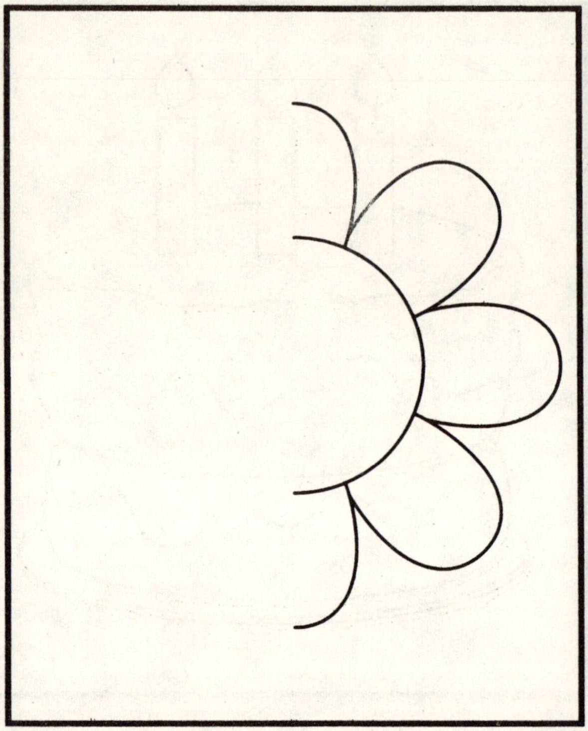

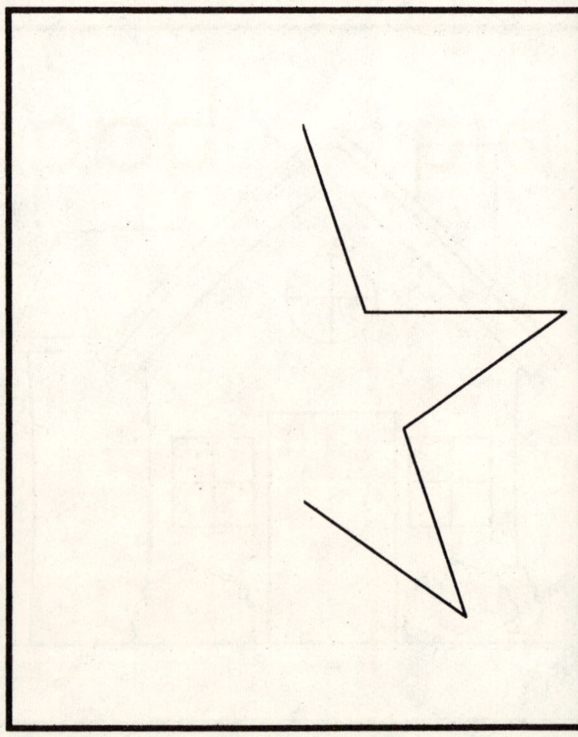

Draw an X on the word in each box that is different.

cab cap cab cab	can can cane can
big bag bag bag	sun sun sun son

Draw an X on the letter or number in each box that is different.

2 2 Z 2	I I I H
t f f f	5 S 5 5

Draw an X on the picture in each box that is different.

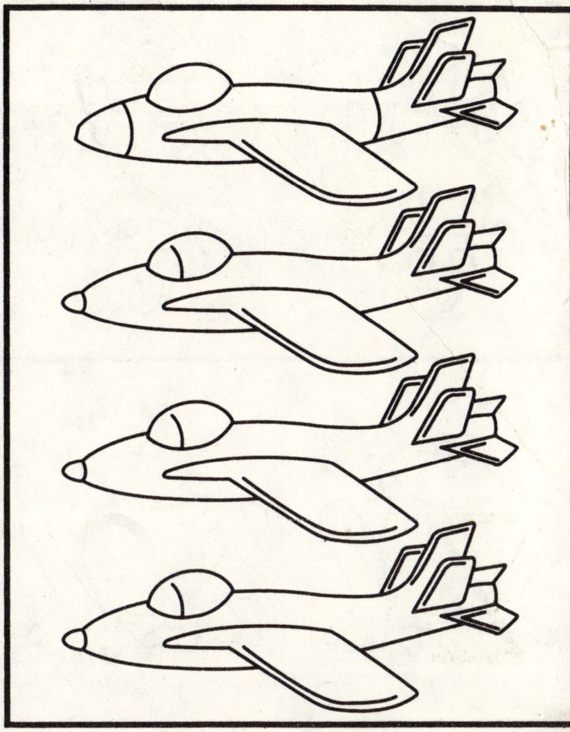

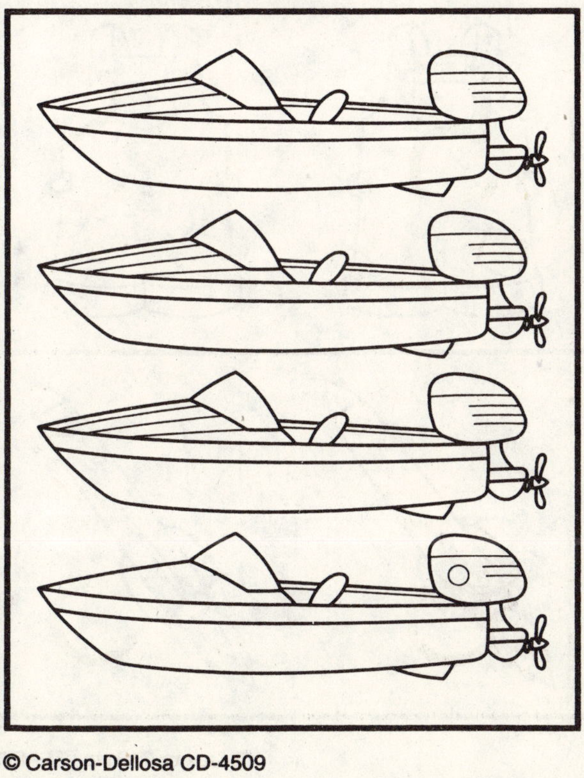

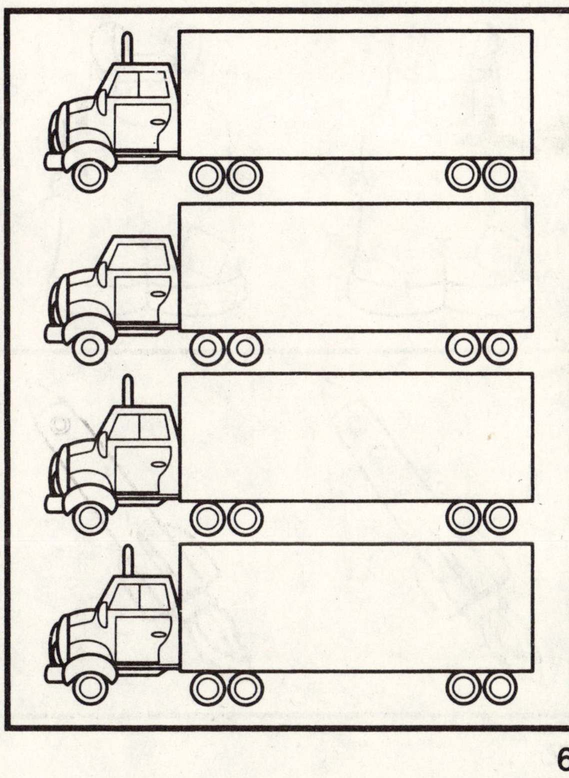

Circle the pictures in each row that are the same. Draw an X on the picture in each row that does not match.

Circle the pictures in each row that are the same. Draw an X on the picture in each row that does not match.

Circle the pictures in each row that are the same. Draw an X on the picture in each row that does not match.